Happy Quarantined Graduation!

A Gift of Verse for Those Graduating During the Weirdest Year Ever

Dear Katie,

Congratulations!!! I am so proud of you! Now just wait until the dust (of the virus) settles to start celebrating big, because you deserve it!

Love you very very much,

Tifi

June 2020

ISBN: 9798639816260

GRADUATION GIFT SERIES

Good Gift Books

Note from the Author

In the Introduction to my other graduation book, "Congratulations to a Graduate," I talked about how much I love attending graduation ceremonies. I discuss how beautiful it is not just to commemorate the achievement, but also the uniqueness of this moment when all these individuals are suspended between two phases of life. I love this aspect of graduation, and I think it's part of what makes the moment so very special.

I was heartbroken when I first heard that graduation ceremonies were being canceled, and I know most graduates were heartbroken, too. Some ceremonies are being held digitally, which is wonderful, but it's not the same. It won't do us any good to pretend it's the same, either. But this moment still deserve recognition, and that is why I decided to pen this verse for graduates during this time of quarantine and social distance.

This situation is deeply unfair to graduates, and I for one hope that we can go the extra mile to make this moment feel just as special for them.

A Deep, Heart-Felt Congratulations to all members of the Quarantined Class of Graduates!

— *Violet Jade*

Dedicated to Brinnlee

A member of the Quarantined Class of Graduates who is very special to me. I can't wait to be in the same room with you again!

It seems a congratulations is due ...

It sounds like someone made it through.

If, in fact, what I heard is true ...

This congratulations belongs to you.

And on most years,
I would give chase ...

And say these words right to your face.

I'd give you a smile, and
a warm embrace ...

And say kind words, to you, with grace.

Just because
the world's been
COVID-19ed ...

Shouldn't take away from what you've achieved.

Through this crisis
I'm sure you've
perceived ...

How all our lives are inter-weaved.

When you consider things, it might appear ...

Unfair this happened on your special year.

It's deeply unfair,
that much is clear ...

You should acknowledge that fact, then persevere.

All that you gained, while pursuing this dream ...

You've learned much — more than it might seem.

Surely, you've learned how to work in a team ...

And how to create an effective meme.

You learned
many different ways
to think ...

When adversity comes, you rise, don't shrink.

You now know life goes by in a blink ...

And how to not get sick if you decide to drink

You know when to read, and when to skim ...

How to boost your mood when things look dim.

The best time of day to hit the gym ...

When to use a word, or its synonym.

Ones like you, so smart and clever ...

The world needs you now more than ever.

You know exactly what you like, however ...

It's typically good to never say never.

As you embark on this adventure new ...

And show us all what you can do.

Just stick to what you know is true ...

And always listen to other points of view.

This year's unpleasantness we can't ignore ...

We can't do restaurants, or even go to a store.

But it doesn't mean we can't adore ...

And celebrate you like never before.

When this thing will end, there's no guarantee ...

Or at least return to normal, to some degree.

On this topic, even experts can't agree ...

Maintaining our sanity, is the only key.

When time comes to return to work ...

We can learn from an era that's so berserk.

We can be more mindful, and less of a jerk ...

Have more appreciation for the grocery clerk.

If this rumor I heard, in fact, is true ...

I heard someone graduated and made it through.

And if that someone, in fact, is you:

A "happy quarantined graduation" is due!

Congratulations to all the graduates out there!!!

We hope you've enjoyed your copy of
Happy Quarantined Graduation

Made in the USA
San Bernardino, CA
24 May 2020